Mike Low is an experienced Quality Trainer, Business Impro. Lead Auditor; he has recently retired from Rolls-Royce plc, having spent a working lifetime involved in manufacturing and quality improvement. He has experience in many different sectors of the Rolls-Royce empire, including Defence Aerospace, Civil Aerospace, and in the Marine and Nuclear sectors. Mike has a Master's degree in The Management of Quality Excellence from Leicester University and a Batchelor's degree [Honours] in English Literature and Humanities from the Open University. Much of Mike's experience has been gained in travelling the world visiting the manufacturing and service providing facilities of many hundreds of Rolls-Royce suppliers. Countries visited include Mexico, USA, Canada, China, Germany, Italy, France and Holland, in addition to all over the UK and Ireland. It is from the experience gained during these visits that the idea for this book was born. He is married to the lovely Deb and lives in Somerset.

THE BLEEDIN' OBVIOUS WAY TO IMPROVE QUALITY IN YOUR BUSINESS

Mike Low

SilverWood

Published by the author in 2013
using SilverWood Books Empowered Publishing ®

SilverWood Books
30 Queen Charlotte Street, Bristol, BS1 4HJ
www.silverwoodbooks.co.uk

ISBN 978-1-78132-145-4 (paperback)
ISBN 978-1-78132-151-5 (ebook)

British Library Cataloguing in Publication Data
A CIP catalogue record for this book is available from the
British Library

Set in Sabon and Futura by SilverWood Books
Printed on responsibly sourced paper

To Deb

Whatever is rightly done, however humble, is noble
Sir Henry Royce

Contents

Preface

This book has been written for people who are new to the practice and application of the basics of good quality or those who want to deepen their knowledge of the basics of good quality.

This book is for you because: you are interested enough to want to read about quality; you want to improve the standing of the business you are in; you are interested in quality of performance, quality of product and quality of service.

This book is designed to give you an easy-to-read guide to the basics of good quality practice. When applied in your business, these basics will lead to improvement. I know this will happen. I know because I have seen it happen throughout my time travelling the world, auditing and leading quality improvement in many different businesses.

Introduction

I do not know what your occupation might be. You may be a shop worker, a managing director, a machinist, a waiter, employed by the National Health Service, a quality manager or a production worker in industry. However, what I do know is that *everything you do matters.*

This book provides guidance on the things that you can do to influence and improve quality of product, quality of service and quality of performance in your business. In these pages the obvious and simple cornerstones of good quality practice are discussed. Case studies that illustrate the benefits of those simple cornerstones are provided with each chapter, some from my own experience, others from sources referenced in the bibliography. Many of these quality cornerstones were found to be missing from numerous manufacturing and service-providing businesses visited in my job role.

Walter Shewhart, the great American quality guru, said in his book, *Economic Control of Quality of Manufactured Product:*

The object of industry is to set up economic ways and means of satisfying human wants, and in so doing to reduce everything possible to routines requiring the minimum amount of human effort.

The obvious and simple quality practices that should require the minimum of human effort are detailed in these pages. When they are followed in your business they will lead to improvements in quality of service, quality of performance and quality of product. These quality practices – when repeatedly stated and encouraged and driven into your business – will become part of your business culture and part of the culture of the people that work within your business. The object of this book is to encourage universal application of the basic, simple and obvious quality practices.

Again, to paraphrase Shewhart:

Economic ways to satisfy human wants with the minimum of human effort.

This is the guiding principle of this book. It should be the guiding principle of every business organisation in the world.

Structure of the book

The book is organised to take readers through the steps of understanding the basics of good quality practice. Each chapter deals with a different topic related to the basics of good quality practice. Each topic has one or more case studies that illustrate the need to apply the basics discussed. One chapter references more advanced 'continual improvement' initiatives that are very important, though not the remit of this book.

Chapter 1

What does the customer want?

It really is obvious

In your business, in any business enterprise, it is vital that customer requirements are known and understood. In order to satisfy these customer requirements it will be necessary for your business to devise a system for manufacturing the product or delivering the service. This system should be written down and appear in the form of printed processes, procedures or practices; or detailed as methods of manufacture or process instructions. These manufacturing instructions, when followed correctly, allow the business to satisfy customer requirements every time. Other forms of manufacturing instructions include: operating instructions, guidance notes and checklists. All define the process required in a series of actions or steps that produce an output.

As an example, take a simple process that you do every day – perhaps making a cup of coffee – and picture writing a checklist of steps that will produce your required output every time. Once the process steps are written down and followed there will be less chance of error, and a consistent output can be produced by everyone who follows the process steps. In other words, you will receive your perfect cup of coffee every time, whoever makes it, provided that everyone follows the process steps.

In addition, having a series of process steps that can be referenced will make improving the manufacturing process easier, as any errors can be corrected and improvements made where necessary.

Standardisation

One of the many good consequences of writing down and recording the preferred method of manufacture is standardisation. Standardisation is important in that it allows universal good quality to flourish through universal application of the preferred and best methods and practices. A good example of the benefits of standardisation is available in any of the global fast-food chains. Go anywhere in the world to an international fast-food outlet and you will almost certainly be served similar food to the same service level. The application of universal best practice provides universal best quality.

Unwritten customer requirements

Where there are no written customer requirements, such as the service level expected by a diner in a restaurant, the service level required is usually unwritten, and consequently more difficult to maintain without well-trained staff. This situation is discussed in more detail in case study 3.

The reality I have seen in many business organisations is that customer requirements that are documented and defined by the customer are often not understood by the people that control the manufacture or delivery of the service. In effect, the customers' requirements are not fully understood and consequently not met. A disappointed customer is usually the result.

Case Study 1
How good are you at reading?

Please answer these questions:
- How many animals of each species did Moses take into the ark?
- Which country has a 4th of July?
- If you take two apples from three apples what do you get?

The answers:
- None (it was Noah who took the animals into the ark)
- All of them
- Two apples

So, how did you do?

Often, people will hurriedly read instructions and statements and jump to incorrect conclusions. In haste, they imagine what is said rather than taking the time to read and properly understand what the words are actually asking to be done. Always take time to read what is being asked of you, and then read it again. When customer instructions are verbal, listen and, if necessary, ask for them to be repeated.

At one time or another, most of us have probably purchased a piece of self-assembly furniture. How would it have been put together without the written instructions? Most written instructions will ensure that the task is completed correctly, in the most efficient way and with the minimum effort.

During many visits to factories and offices, it has not been uncommon to discover a number of well-paid and intelligent individuals who just do not take the trouble to read the customer instructions or take enough notice of what the customer is asking of them. When one asks why, the answer is often, 'I'm too busy,' or, 'That's not my job,' or occasionally just silence. Well, I can tell you (and indeed often told them), that it IS their job, in fact it is the most important part of their job. To understand what the customer wants and to deliver that requirement is pre-eminent to the success of any business.

Case Study 2
Purchasing a magazine
I purchased a new edition of a quarterly magazine containing daily readings just before Christmas, ready to begin reading in the New Year, 2012. It was only when reading began that I noticed this new edition had the date Jan–April, 2011, on its front cover. This date was one year in error. Upon returning this copy

to the place of purchase, I was met with disbelief by the shop assistant, who admitted that he had sold numerous copies, all with the incorrect date. Someone at the store had failed to check a basic requirement of the periodical – that it was up to date when purchasing from the wholesaler – and similarly, so had all the customers who took the periodical home and continued to read it, unaware that it was twelve months out of date.

Case Study 3
Unwritten customer requirements
What is the service level controlling document in a restaurant? No, I've never seen one either. It is invariably unwritten, though if I had my way it would be written down and displayed at the customer entrance. It should read something like this:

Attention Restaurant Staff
Please ensure every time a customer visits our restaurant:
- A member of staff is placed at or near the entrance to the restaurant at all times
- The customer is given a warm and immediate welcome
- Customers are shown to their table
- Fresh water is always available on the table
- Firstly ask: 'May I order you some drinks?'
- Present the menu
- Inform customer of any special dishes available
- Serve food courteously
- Allow reasonable time between courses

- Bill delivered at end of meal when requested by customer
- Ensure the customer is thanked and requested to come again

Obvious, is it not? Surely every restaurant would do this? Well, not with some of the eateries that I have used. At many restaurants it is possible to come away with the impression that the waiters were doing a favour to the diner by serving them.

A recent visit with my family to a local Indian restaurant illustrated the importance of applying the basics of good quality performance. This restaurant was very busy yet it did the basics so well:

- We were greeted at the entrance and showed to a table
- Served in good time with minimum of fuss
- Provided with a jug of water and drinking glasses without asking
- There were enough staff to provide a good level of attention to customers
- We were given a cheerful farewell when leaving the premises and the door was opened for us by a member of staff

Also, during a discussion with the restaurant owner at the conclusion of our meal, we were given a most sparkling quote:

If you can't do it, don't do it. If you can do it, do it well.

Case Study 4

Building St Paul's Cathedral

Sir Christopher Wren built many of the magnificent structures we see in London today (following the Great Fire of 1666), and he used Portland stone for the rebuilding of St Paul's Cathedral, among others. Portland stone was transported from Portland, in Dorset, to London, a journey that took some time in those days. Wren was forever exasperated by the quarrymen of Portland because the quality of the stone they sent him for building was not always as good as expected – some of it was even cracked or stained. Wren would get upset and send it back, causing many delays to his rebuilding programme. One of the reasons Wren often received inferior quality stone was because there was no one at the quarry to tell the quarrymen what was acceptable to him. Had Wren been able to use stone quarried from, say, Southwark, just over the river from St Paul's, he would have been able to tell the quarrymen exactly what was required. The closer proximity of the quarry to the customer would have had an improving effect on the quality of building stone delivered. Had Wren been able to educate the Portland quarrymen more effectively, St Paul's Cathedral would have been built with less trouble.

In business it is no surprise to find many suppliers located near to their major customer. The customer tends to exercise more control over a nearby supplier than one many hundreds or thousands of miles away. Face-to-face communication is much easier and therefore queries are easier to answer and address.

Eventually Wren did take the trouble to travel to Portland and discuss with the quarrymen exactly what he wanted and expected from them. Thereafter, he received what he wanted!

IN A NUTSHELL

Read and listen. Read and listen. Always know exactly what the customer wants.

Chapter 2

Follow your process

Doing the right thing all the time

It has been said that great sportsmen like six-times world snooker champion, Steve Davis, and six-times major golf championship winner, Nick Faldo, were 'boring' to watch. This was not necessarily a reflection of their personality, more a comment upon their ability to do the same thing over and over again with minimal variation. At his playing peak, Nick Faldo would pick up a seven iron and hit a golf ball, say, 147 yards and 9 inches, in a straight line every time. Steve Davis would pick up a snooker cue and make a break of more than fifty every other time. Their performance became boring to some of their audience because of its sameness; because of its lack of variation. Do not underestimate the power of doing the same thing well, over and over again. It is one of the cornerstones of good quality practice.

In large restaurants that serve many hundreds of people every day, line chefs are employed. A line chef's job is to cook the same dish all the time (something popular like chicken jalfrezi or a pepperoni pizza, depending on the restaurant) and to maintain the same standard each time the dish is cooked. It's probably boring to watch the cooking and boring for the chef; however, it's very important that the same standard is maintained – always. If the same standard is not maintained all the time then one poor quality chicken jalfrezi or undercooked pepperoni pizza will lead to a displeased customer who may never return to the restaurant and may tell all his friends about the poor experience. This can lead to less business and therefore reduced profits.

Case Study 5
The basics at war

In his book, *First Light*, the Battle of Britain fighter pilot, Geoffrey Wellum, describes how one of his pilot colleagues was unfortunately killed in his Spitfire because he did not follow the prescribed 'Cockpit Drill'. This was a set of basic instructions designed to ensure that all was as it should be with aircraft and engine prior to take-off. In this case the pilot took off without checking that the directional gyro and artificial horizon instruments were operational. Unfortunately, they were being repaired and were not operational, consequentially making it impossible to fly the aeroplane once airborne. The Spitfire crashed and the pilot died because he did not follow the process and ignored the cockpit drill. This example of non-compliance produced a fatal result. It can be easy to ignore the basics in whatever position one may hold in life. Don't do it.

Case Study 6

Power plants on ocean liners

Ocean liners have power plants that provide the means of propulsion. These power plants contain high-pressure pumps that enable engine-cooling water to be rapidly circulated around the engine, keeping it cool without danger of the cooling water stagnating and consequently allowing the engine to overheat. It is of utmost importance that the pumps work constantly without failure, sometimes for weeks at a time while the liner is at sea. To achieve this demands exceptional reliability from the pump and exceptional quality assurance and quality control by the pump manufacturer.

A cooling pump manufacturer fulfilled all the necessary customer demands to achieve this requisite level of reliability, but with one exception. The manufacturer could not prove that the correct assembly procedure had been carried out during the assembly of the pump. There was no record of what actually took place during the pump assembly process. If a component part within the pump subsequently failed it would be near impossible to determine whether a faulty component or incorrect sequence of assembly caused the failure. Therefore, it would be impossible to carry out an effective and complete root cause analysis, and then take the necessary preventative action to eliminate further failure. Why had this happened? Put simply, the business in question had made the following mistakes:

- Not reading and understanding the customer requirements, which in this case demanded that full and complete assembly records be retained.
- Over-reliance on one individual worker who assembled the pumps from memory without keeping any written records.
- Failure of the customer to ensure that the supplier was following the correct practices demanded by the customer's quality system.
- Failure of the pump manufacturer's management to control their manufacturing processes effectively. In short, the management of the business had lost control of the process.

This situation was corrected, though not without considerable additional time, expense and resource from both customer and supplier. All of this would have been unnecessary had an effective review and understanding of the customer requirements been carried out before manufacturing commenced. In this case the manufacturer needed to write down the assembly process and ensure that it was followed.

Case Study 7
Cleanliness in hospitals
A good example of how following the basics of good practice can produce very worthwhile benefits involves a checklist recently introduced at a number of hospitals in Eastern USA. This intent of this checklist, to be used prior to any surgical operation, was to reduce the incidence of hospital-borne infections. Among the

first instructions on the checklist was 'WASH YOUR HANDS'. The outcry by some surgeons involved in trials of the checklist was considerable. Here were individuals, highly and expensively trained as surgeons over many years, being told to wash their hands as if they were schoolboys. Some found this difficult to accept. Of course, when asked they all said that they always washed their hands prior to performing an operation. Nurses were encouraged to ensure that the surgeons did just that and they used the checklist to enforce the actions required. Subsequent figures showed a reduction in the incidence of hospital-borne infections, thus confirming the importance of washing hands.

IN A NUTSHELL

Have a written process to control all important activity and ensure everyone who needs to follow that process does follow it.

Chapter 3

Education and training

Maximise your most valuable resource: educate yourself and train your people

Training the people in your business is vitally important. Training gives people a greater sense of worth because an interest is being taken in their well-being and in their future. They will feel more valued. Their ability is improved and they become more valuable to the business. The benefits of a well-trained workforce include:

- Consistency across your business
- Best practice from all employees
- Impressed customers

It is important to train staff to be consistent in their approach and in their actions; to say and do the same thing in given situations: when performing manufacturing operations, when delivering a service, when dealing with the public, when serving customers – in any business situation.

Case Study 8

Training of suppliers in the basics of good quality

During a six-year period up to 2012, a two-day supplier training programme was rolled out among the supply chain of a global engineering business. The programme was designed to instil the necessary basic good quality disciplines in the suppliers' business; disciplines that would help to reduce and eventually eliminate the delivery of undeclared non-conformance of product to the global business. Over 2,000 delegates from over 300 business organisations were taken through the two-day course. The training course was applied worldwide among the global businesses supply chain, and from the feedback received from course delegates, the course was a success that led to all-round improvement in supply-chain quality performance.

An interesting side to the aims of the training course concerned the ability of individual delegates to listen and remember instructions issued by the course tutors. Part of the training course included a tick box examination where twenty-five questions required an answer, each question having four Yes or No boxes. The exam guidance explicitly requested that ticks, not crosses, be placed in the boxes. The reason for this was to see if the delegates could follow a simple instruction. The instruction to provide ticks was given twice during the course: once on the first day and again immediately prior to the exam itself. It became a source of amazement to the examination paper markers how so many delegates failed the exam, not through giving incorrect answers, but through answering by using crosses. when the lack of ability to follow this part of the exam process accounted for the majority of failures, it was decided that prior to the exam the presenter would ask all delegates to hold out their right arm and draw a tick in the air. This worked. The incidence of failure through using crosses was eliminated. The over-the-top action of tracing a tick in the air with an outstretched arm was sufficient to instil the correct procedure in the delegates' minds.

Sometimes the exhortation to read, read and read again is not enough. Sometimes people and business organisations have to be led by the hand to process compliance. The story of the ticks and crosses shows that occasionally a simple demonstration can be the answer to ensuring 100% compliance.

Case Study 9
Punctuality on Japanese railways

The following story came from a businessman friend, who travels everywhere by train when in the Far East. My friend happened to notice a Japanese train driver raise and lower his right arm, count to three, and finish by outstretching his arm and pointing his finger in the direction the train was about to travel. Intrigued, the businessman asked a station official why this was done. 'It is part of the process,' was the reply. Does it work? You bet! It gives the train driver a physical action to go with operating the train accelerator and counts down the last three seconds before the train is due to depart – on time, of course.

Beware the rogue operator

Anyone who decides to ignore the agreed and mandated process or method of working without gaining the proper approval first, undermines the work of their colleagues and undermines their business. If someone thinks of a different and possibly better way of doing things then they should be encouraged to highlight their new method and discuss it with a colleague or supervisor. Then, if agreed:

- Obtain approval to introduce the new method
- Trial the new way and measure the results
- Review effectiveness subsequent to full introduction
- Train all the relevant people in the new method

Setting an example – the best way of influencing others

One of the best ways of training and influencing others, thereby minimising the risk of rogue operators, is through setting a good example.

To return briefly to the point made in the introduction: *everything you do matters*. If you are late for work, if you appear indifferent to improving your lot or the lot of others, if you can't be bothered, if your attitude is poor and you are ill-mannered, if your attitude to improvement is negative and one of 'we've always done it this way', someone *will* notice and file your response away for future reference. And of course, the higher up the ladder of life you happen to be, more notice will be taken of your actions and more will be made of your lapses. Always set a good example. Go out of your way to do so. It will pay dividends in the end. Even if you are unaware of the consequences of your actions, there will be consequences, and they will affect your business and your position.

Setting an example is not the main means of influencing another, it is the only means.

Albert Einstein

Case Study 10
Independence of inspection
Some manufacturing business organisations in industry employ third-party (that is, neither their own nor their customers') inspection companies to verify the manufactured product. This is not necessarily the best way to ensure that the product is produced correctly, because third-party agency personnel will never be as familiar with the product as those that make it or those that purchase it. From my own experience, a supplier of cast metallic product employed third-party inspection. This was at their customer's insistence, following poor quality performance. This imposition lasted for over a year and the following is a situation discovered during a visit to the supplier:

The third-party inspector was located in the manufacturing area, adjacent to the supplier's inspectors for the duration of the imposition. In time, the third-party inspector took on the culture and methods of the supplier inspectors whose work he was there to oversee. He fell into the supplier's routines and the improving effect he was supposed to have did not take place. Independence of action was lost. In other words, the inspector 'went native'.

To save time the third-party inspector was using pre-printed checklists, upon which all the major inspection points in the manufacturing process were already ticked as being correct *before they were actually checked*. This nullified the effect of using the checklist and was liable to produce an attitude among the third-party inspector of pre-judgement.

The third-party inspector had failed in a basic duty, which was to set an example to all the supplier inspectors of the correct way to carry out the job in hand.

This situation was corrected and improved by retraining the relevant personnel in the basics of good inspection techniques. And, of course, the abandonment of pre-printed ticked checklists.

IN A NUTSHELL

People will perform better if an interest is taken in their future; if they are given training and are set a good example.

Chapter 4

Simplify, simplify

Again, simplify

Following a recent upgrade to my business laptop, I was not in the least surprised to find that many of the operations in the various applications now took more clicks on the mouse to perform than previously. What was going on? The system had apparently become more complex. Why make something more time-consuming than necessary? Programmers are very clever, but why not try and make things easier? For most people, using a computer in their job role is standard, so why not make the various systems operate through using fewer clicks on a mouse? This could well reduce sources of error and allow speedier responses and report writing.

It has been a frustrating experience to see just how unnecessarily complex people can make everyday things which are necessary to the successful operation of a business.

Suppliers, beware of customer instructions

Customers can be a cause of poor quality when they give suppliers poor product definition or poor instructions.

In both manufacturing and service businesses it is important that the customer should tell the supplier exactly what is required. These requirements should be cascaded to the supplier in as simple a way as possible. If this is not done and the requirements are unnecessarily complex or difficult, then it is more likely that there will be poor delivery and poor quality.

Customers' instructions to suppliers should be as short as possible with the minimum of words and detail. Needlessly complex instructions may lead to difficulties in understanding. Sometimes the complexity of defining the customer requirements reaches unmanageable limits. In one instance of my experience, the amount of paper needed to define the customer requirements for a *single* component weighed 2kg. The paper was weighed in order to save time counting the pages!

Customers must make sure requirements are clear and concise and understood by the supplier. Effort put in at the start of a contract between customer and supplier will pay dividends at the end.

Case Study 11
The obvious requirements of inspection
Many customers ask their suppliers to ensure and guarantee that the following are in place before delivering their product to the customer:

- The product has been inspected for conformance to customer requirements before delivery
- The person performing the inspection is suitably trained and experienced

- This suitably trained and experienced person has good eyesight (through evidence of a regular eye test)
- The inspection is undertaken in an area that is adequately illuminated for inspection

Why would any competent business organisation not do these basic things? Well, the reason basics are often demanded in the contract between customer and supplier is that many suppliers do not carry out these obvious fundamentals of inspection. Experience has proved that when they are not followed every time, the result is often delivery of a non-conforming product.

All forms of written business communication can and should be as brief and as simple as possible while retaining the required meaning. Good grammar is also important. Businesses have recently begun issuing 'Good Writing Guides'. These are designed to encourage employees to write in a professional, lucid and clear manner, and can be very useful in ensuring that good standards of communication are maintained.

IN A NUTSHELL

Complexity is the enemy of reliability. Simplify your business processes and methods of working as much as possible.

Chapter 5

Quality policy

The importance of applying a guiding quality principle

My experiences in over 250 manufacturing and service organisations around the world, in Canada, USA, Mexico, China, France, Germany, Holland, Italy, Ireland and all around the UK, show that the overwhelming majority of employees, when asked, 'What is your company's Quality Policy?' reply, 'I don't know.' This situation can, and should, be remedied by ensuring that the Quality Policy:

- Is short and to the point
- Is written without jargon or unnecessary 'management speak'
- Contains a memorable phrase that is easily remembered
- Is well advertised throughout the organisation through effective visual management
- Is audited to ensure that it is effectively 'flowed down' throughout the business

The following is typical of the kind of Quality Policy that manufacturing businesses issue today:

ABC manufacturing is a long-term business and we continually invest in facilities, technology and people so that we can constantly improve the quality and efficiency of our products. We have accumulated a vast amount of data, experience and knowledge that enables us to continually improve effectiveness in our processes. These processes are embedded in our Quality Management System, which is applied across the business and in all of our operations. Continuous improvement is essential to meet rising expectations of our customers and to remain competitive. It requires technology and teamwork. The pursuit of excellence means working together and complying with agreed processes, across businesses and functions.

Well, having read it, would you remember it? Even more, what is it actually saying to you about quality?

None of the interviewed personnel employed by this business could quote more than three words from it. What is the point of having a Quality Policy that very few remember and is uninspiring? If it is not memorable, it is unlikely to make individuals in that business become more devoted to improving quality.

During the research for this chapter, I reviewed

many Quality Policies from a range of business types. It was interesting to discover that some businesses do not have a recognisable Quality Policy, even some of those with ISO 9001 certification. Indeed, some of the Quality Policies researched ran to over 1,000 words!

The following examples of Quality Policies further illustrate the importance of lucidity and succinctness.

G4S plc Quality Policy

- Commitment Driving
  Provide resources and promote all the decisions necessary for meeting the Quality Programs of our company.
- Continuous Improvement
  Promote continuous improvement of processes through regular program review and the continuing role of the experiences of our staff.
- Human Resources Management and Technology
  Ensure professionalism, expertise and staff training and promote the ongoing search for the best technologies to manage our operations.
- Organization
  Offer a versatile organizational structure, so that there is responsiveness to the giddy tone of our operations.
- Legality
  Comply with laws relating to all activities carried out by G4S, promoting among its members, suppliers, subcontractors and consultants, conduct based on ethical principles and transparent attitudes.

Maybe a little too long to be memorable.

Honeywell Quality Policy

Right the first time, every time – in all aspects of the business. Tools like Six Sigma help achieve that goal.

Concise and to the point, and almost where we want to be. Even more succinct is this:

Error is Horror!

Brief, straight to the point, inspiring, memorable and impressive. This Quality Policy belongs to the Mumbai Dabbawallas, who deliver 200,000 hot packed lunches to office workers by 12.45 every day. They deliver one million Tiffin boxes per week in India's largest city and have a delivery failure rate of one Tiffin box not reaching its destination on time every six weeks. One in six million! How do they do it? Each Dabbawalla has to commit to a 30,000 rupee investment and thereafter shares in the profits of the organisation. It is in their interest that all customers are satisfied all the time. They achieve this phenomenal success rate by emphasising the facets of belonging and pride. Error is Horror! Error produces dissatisfied customers which may lead to loss of business and less profit, which could then lead to a loss of jobs.

If your business has not ensured that all personnel know and understand the business Quality Policy, then an opportunity for business improvement is being lost. An effective method of driving the Quality Policy into the culture of a business is by printing the Quality Policy on the reverse of individuals' business cards. This has the advantage of ensuring that the Quality Policy is not overlong and therefore more easily remembered.

A recent visit to a bearing manufacturer in the Midlands showed the good effect of having a short and memorable Quality Policy. The Quality policy is taught to personnel through Induction Training, where new starters are educated on its importance. All business cards had the Quality Policy printed on the reverse, reinforcing the message with employees and customers. Also, working areas had good visual management, where the Quality Policy is displayed prominently. That Quality Policy is:

Quality is the cornerstone of our reputation and is central to the ability of each business to achieve its mission.

This is backed up by written responsibilities and expectations for each employee.

The ISO standard 9001 is explicit in what is required from businesses that hold certification. ISO 9001 section 5.3: Quality Policy states:

Top management shall ensure that the quality policy:
Is appropriate to the purpose of the organization
Includes a commitment to comply with requirements and continually improve the effectiveness of the quality management system
Is communicated and understood within the organization
Is reviewed for continuing suitability

The Midlands bearing manufacturing business is one of only three business organisations I have visited since 2000 that were found to be compliant with all the above ISO requirements.

It is one thing to have a Quality Policy, another to have objective evidence that ensures that it is cascaded through the business. How can you be sure that this happens and is providing useful guidance to personnel? Auditing the process of distribution of the Quality Policy would highlight deficiencies and facilitate improvement. Some characteristic questions to ask when one needs to be sure that the Quality Policy is being circulated throughout the business are:

- Does your business have a Quality Policy or a mission, values or purpose statement?
- Are these statements built into your management system?
- What do you wish to achieve from your organisation and its management system?
- How does the policy link to the organisation's goals, aims and objectives?
- What measures are in place to ensure consistency?
- What reports or measures are available that tell you the business is delivering the requirements of the top-level statements?

These points may seem apparent, yet very few businesses in my experience ensure that the Quality Policy of the company is cascaded effectively. Often the Quality Policy is something that is displayed prominently at the entrance foyer to the main office or factory, and ignored everywhere else.

IN A NUTSHELL

Ensure your Quality Policy is to the point and that the most important message fits on the back of a business card; it must be known and understood by all who work in the business and can be audited as applicable throughout the organisation.

Chapter 6

Continuity

Doing the same thing, whoever is in control

> *The average length of time in office for ministers of education since the First World War is less than two years...It has got to change. Under Labour, it will, I want my ministers to expect to take responsibility for seeing a strategy through.*
>
> Tony Blair, December 1996

Blair appointed five Secretaries of State for Education in his tenure as Prime Minister. An average of...two years!

I have seen too many examples of people achieving senior positions in which they do not intend to remain for any longer than it takes to make a 'quick hit', i.e. to impress superiors as quickly as possible with a business improvement initiative, which more often than not contributes little or nothing to the long-term overall effectiveness of a business. They then leave, usually before the full effects of their newly introduced changes are felt, having sought another role in the belief that their success is measured by continuous movement upwards through different roles.

Please, let the campaign for greater continuity in management positions start now!

Case Study 12

Continuity

An engineering services business supplier was visited twice within ten months. Two teams of engineers, one supplier, one customer, were engaged in introducing an important new method of manufacture and were in constant communication, often meeting at both the supplier and the customer premises. At the first visit to the supplier the names of the two engineering teams were recorded. At the return visit ten months later, it was discovered that all the customer engineering team had either moved to different roles or left the customer's employ. Surely some of the original customer team should have been retained, at least to provide the continuity that comes from getting to know someone! Conversely, the supplier engineering team had only one change from the previous visit.

The complete change of personnel in the customer engineering team did not help with the smooth running and completion of an important project.

In my experience visiting small, medium and large business enterprises all over the world, it was common for many managers in the small and medium businesses to be resident in their management position for far longer than in corresponding roles in large businesses. A sample survey showed that the average term in the small and medium businesses was eleven years. A much shorter 'time in role' emerged in the larger businesses that employed more people.

In other words, the bigger the business, the more likely an increased frequency of turnover in management positions. And not just in management positions – often other roles, particularly in purchasing departments, would have similar turnover rates. Consequently, in the larger businesses, continuity was more difficult to maintain and the smooth running of business initiatives was often not consistent. A newly introduced manager would tend to modify the approach to an ongoing project. This often resulted in confusion among those involved in the project.

When a change in the internal culture of a business is sought, the persistent application and repetition of the culture change agenda will be necessary. This will be helped through having the same person or people managing the change. It is more likely that people affected by the sought change will have greater belief if they can see that the leaders of change are in it to the end.

Of course, it is not just management or engineering roles that benefit from continuity. Advantages come from ensuring continuity in many areas.

Case Study 13

Maintenance of inspection standards

A recent visit to a sheet metal fabricator that manufactures metal cabinets showed the importance of ensuring continuity. Many of the cabinets made by this business were painted in the colour demanded by the customer. After painting, cabinets were inspected to ensure the paint finish was of an acceptable standard, with no blemishes, poor paint adherence, scratches or surface irregularities. The paint inspection was performed by a full-time inspector. I was told by the inspector's supervisor that production decreased when the inspector was on holiday or off with sickness 'because the painted cabinets would wait for inspection until the inspector returned and was able to inspect them.' This of course would ensure that a consistent standard of paint finish was maintained. However, the effects on productivity when the inspector was away did not seem to be considered. I suggested that a visual acceptance standard for paint finishes be compiled, including photographs of acceptable and unacceptable finishes, and, where necessary, physical representations of acceptable paint finishes. This could be done with the inspector's help. This would then allow other inspectors to carry out the paint inspection role to the same acceptance standard. This was then done. Obvious? Of course! Yet it was only completed when it was pointed out to the business how much it would decrease disruption and interruption of output.

IN A NUTSHELL

What is needed, ideally, is a person who can take a proposal from conception to reality, work the long hours, build a team, handle the pressures and setbacks, manage technical and people problems alike, and stick with the effort for years on end without getting distracted or leaving all in mid-stream to further their career.

The Checklist Manifesto, **Atul Gawande**

Chapter 7

Human Factors

Why things can go wrong

This chapter discusses human factors. That is, those human characteristics that make us all human. There have been a number of research projects into what they are and why they happen, most notably by organisations such as the Civil Aviation Authority, the US Federal Aviation Authority and British Rail. Your business should be aware of them and where necessary, take action to correct any failings in human factors. Guidance and suggestions on correcting failings are given below.

The following is a quote from 'CAA Safety Regulations Group CAP715: An introduction to Aircraft Maintenance Engineering Human factors for JAR 66':

> *If everyone could be persuaded to acknowledge Murphy's Law* – [anything that can go wrong, will go wrong] – *this might help overcome the 'it will never happen to me' belief that many*

people hold. It is not true that accidents only happen to people who are irresponsible or 'sloppy'. Incidents and accidents described show that errors can be made by experienced, well-respected individuals and accidents can occur in organisations previously thought to be 'safe'.

Following the publication of the CAA report, human factors training became compulsory in repair and overhaul of aircraft and aircraft engines. Human factors departments exist in the nuclear industry, railway industry and other business organisations where safety and safe operation of product are of paramount concern.

What are the most important and relevant human factors? Much of the research carried out concluded that there are twelve. They became known as the 'Dirty Dozen'. I would actually describe them as the 'Baker's Dozen' because there are actually thirteen:

Human Factors: The Baker's Dozen
1. Lack of Communication
2. Complacency
3. Lack of Knowledge
4. Distraction
5. Lack of Teamwork
6. Fatigue
7. Lack of Resource
8. Pressure
9. Lack of Assertiveness

10. Stress
11. Lack of Awareness
12. Norms
13. Lack of Consequences

Each of these human factors is defined here together with suggested mitigating factors.

Lack of Communication

Signs include: poor written and oral communication; poor level of detail in communication; poor team communication and underdeveloped communication practices.

Mitigation: be aware of communication barriers such as noise, language, culture or perceptions. Listen actively. Focus on what is being said. Consider how you say what you say; for example, use of body language or tone of voice – these all send signals. Always check that the recipient has understood the message.

Complacency

Signs include: poor attention to detail; loss of interest in job role and lack of enthusiasm.

Mitigation: diversification through change in job role and retraining.

Lack of Knowledge

Signs include: reluctance to act; avoidance of decision making; passing responsibility onto others and taking a 'what do you think?' approach.

Mitigation: expect change, plan for it, anticipate it

and take time to acquire knowledge for new ways of working. Provide support for people lacking knowledge.

Distraction

Signs include: inattentiveness; willingness to do any task other than own; flitting between tasks and leaving tasks incomplete.

Mitigation: use a detailed checklist for critical tasks; back up a step – after a distraction, go back a step when you return to work. When others distract you, politely tell them you are busy – it is OK to inform people that you don't wish to be interrupted and need to concentrate.

Lack of Teamwork

Signs include: duplication of tasks; tasks not completed, resulting in frustration and wasted effort.

Mitigation: improve communication – the importance of effective communication cannot be overemphasised. In order for teams to work well, everyone must know what is going on; roles should be clarified and expectations understood. It is essential to listen and give others the opportunity to express their views and concerns.

Fatigue

Signs include: short attention span; forgetfulness; constant yawning; lack of attention to detail and slowness of response.

Mitigation: ensure a good night's sleep; take exercise;

ask others to check your work; change the task you are doing; go for a walk around and review your work environment.

Lack of Resources
Signs include: cutting corners; failure to meet deadlines and rarely finishing a task.

Mitigation: identify alternative human resources and know who can provide backup with the required skill sets; investigate the streamlining of processes to reduce time-wasting.

Pressure (time pressure and deadlines)
Signs include: cutting corners; supervisor and managerial time pressures cascaded onto individuals.

Mitigation: communicate your concerns and ask for help. Ensure pressure isn't self-induced by reviewing time management and prioritising tasks; conditions change, so verify your assumption. Just say no if there is a serious risk that the work will not be done correctly.

Lack of Assertiveness
Signs include: succumbing to pressure when inappropriate, for example, giving in too readily when you may be convinced that a course of action is wrong; someone who can't say 'NO'.

Mitigation: refuse to compromise your standards; employ your own quality skills and act upon them if you see non-compliance. Avoid self-censorship – being the devil's advocate can open up a group view and provide new insights.

Stress

Signs include: denial when confronted with evidence of wrongdoing; dealing with minor tasks instead of major tasks; shortness of temper; inability to concentrate; any one or a combination of tiredness, sickness and absence.

Mitigation: take a break from the task; break down large tasks, making them easier to do; be aware of the things that are causing stress and think of them as things that can be dealt with confidently.

Lack of Awareness

Signs include: failure to realise the consequences of actions; absence of perception and absence of knowledge.

Mitigation: ask others to inspect work done; review work instructions to ensure compliance. If in doubt, ask, or check the appropriate documentation. People 'don't know what they don't know'. If still in doubt: STOP.

Norms: 'We've always done it this way'

Signs include: formal practices and policies differing from the usual custom and practice – the two should be the same; unusable procedures; danger of cutting corners. Where unofficial norms exist they can lead to a breakdown in process compliance.

Be aware that there are official and unofficial norms:

Unofficial Norms: Usually apparent from liberal use of the following phrases: 'my way', 'tribal knowledge', 'just do it', 'group way', 'this is how we do it in this department', 'we've always done it this way'.

Official Norms: These are the policies, procedures, work instructions and manuals that make sure a business organisation's processes comply with all customer requirements.

Mitigation – Unofficial Norms: Provide a channel for creativity; channel ideas to the appropriate department. When people feel they are not being listened to they may try their ideas without proper authorisation. Remember your personal power – don't be pressured into doing something that conflicts with procedures.

Official Norms: Read, read and read again; review your reference documents; notify people of changes. Most people tend to think it's business as usual unless they are told otherwise. Make procedures and instructions easy to find and use.

Lack of Consequences

Signs include: failure of an individual or group to complete a process action because there are no consequences whether the action is completed or not, i.e. no praise when successful and no censure when unsuccessful. In short, the people performing the process have no expectation that anything will happen, irrespective of what they do. Other signs of Lack of Consequences are: anarchy; inconsistency; lack of awareness of procedures; process breakdown; the adoption of a 'who cares' attitude; liberal use of the following phrases: 'why bother?', 'it doesn't matter' and, 'I couldn't care less'. Loss of interest in role or project; knowingly doing things incorrectly and not following the process.

Mitigation: Insist that the correct processes or practices are followed; ensure that there are consequences if actions are not completed; give praise when actions are completed satisfactorily.

Case Study 14

The Tenerife Aeroplane Disaster

This disaster had the highest number of fatalities of any single accident in aviation history, resulting in the death of 583 people.

The Tenerife disaster took place on March 27, 1977, when two Boeing 747 airliners collided at Los Rodeos Airport on the island of Tenerife. The aircraft involved were Pan Am Flight 1736, and KLM Flight 4805.

KLM 4805, taking off on the only runway of the airport, crashed into the Pan Am aircraft, which was taxiing on the same runway. Visibility was severely limited at the time due to fog.

Lined up for take-off, the KLM crew received a clearance to fly a certain route immediately after take-off. Due to the fog, the KLM crew was not able to see the Pan Am 747 taxiing on the runway ahead of them. In addition, neither of the aircraft could be seen from the control tower and the airport was not equipped with runway radar.

While the KLM crew had started its take-off run, the KLM Flight Engineer repeatedly expressed his concern about the Pan Am 747 not being clear of the runway, but he was overruled by the captain.

Consequently take-off was not interrupted.

The accident had a lasting influence on the industry, particularly in the area of communication. An increased emphasis was placed on using standardised phraseology in ATC communication by both controllers and pilots alike, thereby reducing the risk of misunderstandings. As part of these changes, the word 'take-off' was removed from general usage, and is only spoken by ATC when actually clearing an aircraft to take off. Flight crew members were encouraged to challenge their captains when they believed something was not correct, and captains were instructed to listen to their crew and evaluate all decisions in light of crew concerns. This concept would later be expanded into what is known as Crew Resource Management training, which is now mandatory for all airline pilots.

Awareness of human factors is very important. Not all organisations need to be as aware, or employ mitigation to the extent of businesses such as those in the nuclear industry or the national railway network, where safety considerations may far exceed those of something like a restaurant. However, all business organisations can learn from them and improve their business accordingly.

It is worth noting that the Tenerife disaster was not caused by just one human factor, rather it was a combination of many: lack of assertiveness, lack of communication, pressure, lack of teamwork, and so on. When things do go wrong, it is almost always due to a combination of human factors.

Case Study 15

Car parking

A good example of a lack of consequences relates to car parking in a town centre near my home. There are several parking restrictions in place, such as double yellow lines and 'No Parking' signs. However, many people park their cars in illegal and awkward places: next to traffic lights, on zebra crossings or at the edge of T-junctions. Why do they do that? Because in their experience, parking restrictions are very rarely enforced. If authorities do not enforce parking restrictions and there are no traffic wardens available, some people will break the law with impunity. Because there are no consequences to the action of illegal parking, it becomes a penalty-free crime. When a required process or action is not followed and there are no consequences, people will often determine that the process can be altered to suit.

IN A NUTSHELL

Be aware of human factors. They will affect your business.

Chapter 8

How to improve quality

Ask yourself this question

During the research for this book, the following question was posed to a number of quality managers, supply chain managers and others in quality-related roles in industry: What is the biggest single thing your business organisation can do to improve quality?

Some of the shorter, more enlightening and probably more obvious answers were:

'Accept change'
Only through accepting change can quality be improved; only by accepting change can a business move forward and improve. Only through accepting change will an individual become more efficient and a more useful and capable person.

'Develop your people'
Train and encourage your people to be better, to improve and therefore enrich your organisation.

'Follow your process'

Achieve the best process in your business and by following it, you control production and you control the service provided, keeping the customer happy.

'Change people or change people'

Again, improve quality through acceptance of change. If your people will not accept change, or they show themselves unable to improve the process or themselves, then your business will suffer.

'Change behaviours/change culture'

This same message was consistently made by a succession of quality managers. A successful business is made through its people, who, if they can change and improve themselves and the processes/services provided, will take the business to new levels of success.

'Employ more people in the Quality Department'

This is a common plea from quality managers, and from many people who also work at the 'coal face' of quality (inspectors, quality engineers and supplier quality engineers).

'Sack the MD/Production Manager/Mr X/ Mrs Y, etc.'

A sad comment that shows the occasional gulf between those who practise and drive quality performance and those who operate as production managers or are responsible for the delivery of a product or service within a business. I understand the need to deliver a product or service on time and to cost. It is probably worth remembering, however, what Thomas Jefferson said: 'Delay is preferable to error.'

Case Study 16
Laptop battery failure

Many business organisations measure their quality performance in PPM (parts per million). That means, for example, if twenty-five items are defective through poor quality from a total deliverable quantity of 1,000 items, then the defective PPM would be 25,000. In 2006-2007, the Sony Corporation had the task of recalling eight million laptop batteries that were suspected of being faulty. Poor quality control had resulted in eighteen recorded instances of battery failure. Some batteries caught fire while in use, in one instance causing a laptop to catch fire while being used on a passenger aircraft. Eighteen failures in eight million give a PPM figure of 2.25. In most businesses this figure would be acclaimed as exemplary, yet the costs of battery recall and the accompanying adverse publicity meant that the negative effect on Sony Corporation's bottom line in 2007 was measured in millions of dollars.

Case Study 17
The Hubble Space Telescope

An instance of the importance of performing a 'basic reality check', concerns the Hubble Space Telescope. This telescope, deployed in outer space, orbiting the Earth, has led to a significant growth in man's knowledge of the universe. It was not without teething problems, however. Almost immediately after Hubble went into orbit, it became clear that something was wrong.

The telescope's primary mirror had a flaw. It was slightly the wrong shape, causing the light that bounced off the centre of the mirror to focus in a different place from the light bouncing off the edge. This tiny flaw was enough to distort the view. The engineers had a solution: a series of small mirrors could be used to intercept the light reflecting off the mirror, correcting the flaw and bouncing the light to the telescope's instruments. The correction device could be installed by astronauts and correct the images produced.

Astronauts and NASA staff spent eleven months training. The subsequent space mission successfully corrected the flaws in the telescope.

This story is a triumph in overcoming a set of very difficult circumstances. However, the correction cost millions of dollars! All of which would have been unnecessary if a basic reality check – to test the telescope for effectiveness before its launch into space – had been carried out prior to launch. This would seem obvious yet it was not done.

IN A NUTSHELL

'Eternal vigilance' must be your watchwords. Do it right all the time.

Chapter 9

Continual improvement

Keeping ahead of the opposition

Having discussed the basics of good quality practice that should be embedded within the culture of your business, it is now important to pay some attention to continual improvement. I would hasten to add here that this book is definitely not a guide to the many continual improvement doctrines freely available. The philosophies and practices of Kaizen and Six Sigma – with their 'Define, Measure, Analyse, Improve, Control' philosophy; Advanced Product and Quality Planning or Production Part Approval Process, etc. – are important and very relevant to all businesses. They are for other volumes, however. Our primary concern here is that quality basics come first and continual improvement follows thereafter.

In order for any business to improve and progress, the application of continual improvement throughout the business is a necessity. If a business does not improve quickly enough or well enough, then it will find it difficult to survive. One of the benefits of continual improvement can be seen by considering the longevity of a gas turbine engine over a forty-year period.

Average number of hours a gas turbine could fly before it would be liable to failure:

- 1965 – 2,500
- 1985 – 17,500
- 1995 – 100,000
- 2005 – 165,000
  Source: US Federal Aviation Authority

The growth in civilian air travel over the last forty years posed many problems for planners in the 1970s. One question given a great deal of thought by those planners was, 'What if the rate of occurrence of civil aircraft incidents and accidents per number of flights was maintained, in future times, at 1970s levels?'

Projecting forward the very large increase in passenger air traffic, it was realised that with 1970s levels of incidents per flight, it would be likely that an aeroplane-related event would occur every week sometime in the future. In the face of the weekly reporting of aircraft engine failure or even worse, a weekly passenger aircraft crash, passenger confidence would be liable to decline – this would result in people thinking twice before using air transport.

Consequently, it was apparent to 1970s planners that improvements in quality performance and reliability would be fundamental in maintaining customer confidence as the number of passenger flights increased. Therefore, quality of product in the aerospace industry was, and continues to be, continually improved.

Similar improvement in quality can be found for all man-made devices that have become more reliable and are of better quality than ever before.

Case Study 18

The Apollo space programme

An example of applying continual improvement in quality and reliability comes from the USA National Aeronautics and Space Administration Apollo Programme that was carried out during the 1960s and 1970s. This was the programme designed to put men on the moon. One of the biggest problems faced by the management of the programme concerned the tens of thousands of component parts that had to work if the mission was to succeed. Each of these individual parts was required, by the programme managers, to have a reliability rating of 0.99999 – only one possible failure in 100,000 opportunities. This is a failure rate of 10 Parts per Million. There was no way to subject each of those tens of thousands of parts to individual testing and still complete the mission within the decade. Instead of using this as a reason to extend the project deadline, the management of the Apollo programme decided, in consultation with the project engineers, that it wasn't necessary to test all those component parts to ensure their compliance with requirements. The view was taken that if an individual part was designed correctly and built exactly to NASA specifications, it would work as designed every time. Accordingly, the degree of supplier control, audit and surveillance was increased and suppliers were instructed to follow the manufacturing process correctly and inspect each component 100%, thereby ensuring the component parts were correct in all instances. The validity of this approach was confirmed by the successful launching of Apollo II and the return to Earth of the astronauts who first set foot upon the moon.

In terms of productivity and quality performance measured in recent times, one of the most successful car manufacturing plants in Europe is the Nissan manufacturing facility in Sunderland. The management at this plant have introduced Japanese-style quality improvement initiatives that have revolutionised production and to which the workforce have responded. Initiatives introduced include the doctrine of Kaizen, or continual improvement by which everyone is encouraged to improve their working environment, no matter how small, in order to make it more productive or workable. Every department has its own Kaizen team.

Continual improvement is crucial to building a successful business, and should be applied where necessary and where relevant. It must be built on a solid foundation, however. That solid foundation is provided by the basics of good quality practice being in place and followed every time, all the time. Improvement initiatives like Kaizen or Six Sigma are of little value if introduced into an organisation where the basics of good quality practice are not deep-rooted and applied consistently and permanently.

There are many business improvement methods used in industry today. The chances of success for such methods are increased when the basics of good quality practice are applied all the time.

Obstacles to following the basics

The idea for this book was born partly from the frustration of often seeing how the basics of good quality practice were forgotten, ignored or pushed aside in the pursuit of seemingly higher level quality improvement initiatives. These were often:

- Not given enough thought and appropriate planning
- Not given enough consultation with people affected by the improvement
- Perceived as being necessary without actually understanding what the customer required
- Not seen through to a satisfactory conclusion

The basics of good quality practice can be forgotten and ignored when individuals believe that good quality practice has become unnecessary or has outlived its usefulness. Those employees responsible for the maintenance of standards must ensure their application all the time.

IN A NUTSHELL

Always ensure the basics of good quality practice are continually applied and followed. Then seek to improve your business.

Chapter 10

Conclusions

Think again

It is obvious that the customer should be given what they are asking for; that people in your business should be adequately trained and their skills developed; that good processes to control manufacturing or manage services should be established and followed all the time by whoever is performing them. It may also seem obvious to make sure that your business has a quality policy that is relevant, memorable and known by the relevant people. And of course, a good example must be set by all in your business – if anyone decides to operate outside of the agreed process and ignores the agreed practice, there must be consequences to their actions, whether good or bad. It is also important to keep business practices and processes as simple as possible and avoid complexity. Yes, all this is obvious. Why then do so many business organisations not follow many of the simple and effective good quality practices discussed here? Why do so many businesses find themselves struggling to satisfy customers as a consequence of not following the basic cornerstones of good quality, and the basics of good quality practice?

There are many reasons why. It is possible that a lot of people in business may well be unaware of the basic cornerstones that have been discussed here. My hope is that their discussion in this book will influence you to the extent that you are motivated to push forward and advocate their permanent application within your business.

I sincerely hope your business benefits from reinforcing the practices we have discussed. Please remember the reinforcement and continual application of the basics of good quality is a permanent affair and cannot just be a nine-day wonder. To be successful a business must embed the basic quality practices, applying them all the time. Only when that is achieved should those basic quality practices be built upon through application of the many more in-depth business improvement initiatives widely available.

Finally, to repeat the maxim of Walter Shewhart:

The object of industry is to set up economic ways and means of satisfying human wants and in so doing to reduce everything possible to routines requiring a minimum amount of human effort.

Every business organisation in the world should be seeking to satisfy their customers with the minimum of human effort. That is not to cut corners, take risks or to deliver an inferior product or service. Rather, it is to seek the most efficient and effective way of doing business. It is to build on the cornerstones of good quality practice to improve the business and stay ahead of competition. It is to do the right thing all the time.

Bibliography

Shewhart, W. *The Economic Control of Quality of Manufactured Product*, D. Van Nostrand Co, 1931.

Parris, M. and Mason, P. *Mission Accomplished*, JR Books, 2007.

Wellum, G. *First Light*, Penguin, 2003.

Gawande, Atul. *The Checklist Manifesto*, Profile Books, 2009.

Dryburgh, Alastair. *Everything You Know About Business is Wrong*, Headline Book Publishing, 2011.

Marshall, Don R. *The Four Elements of Successful Management*, Amacom division of American Management, 1999.

Quality World, The Chartered Quality Institute, various editions, 2009–2013.

Parris, Matthew and Bryson, Andrew. *Parting Shots*, Penguin, 2010.

Various Quality Policies from different organisations (named in the text 2011–2013 – all are in the public domain)

CAA Safety Regulations Group CAP715 'An introduction to Aircraft Maintenance Engineering Human factors for JAR 66', published in January 2001.

AS9100C Quality Management Systems – Requirements for Aviation, Space and Defence Organizations. Published by SAE.

The Tenerife Airport Disaster 1977, Wikipedia and other sources, May 2013.

'We Have a Problem': the story of the deployment of the Hubble Space Telescope, Google, 26 January 2011.

Find out more at mikelow.co.uk